REV. SR. IMMACULATA

Our lady of Guadalupe novena and biography

Prayers of Mother of Civilization of Love, Hope, and Salvation.

Copyright © 2023 by Rev. Sr. Immaculata

All rights reserved. No part of this publication may be reproduced, stored or transmitted in any form or by any means, electronic, mechanical, photocopying, recording, scanning, or otherwise without written permission from the publisher. It is illegal to copy this book, post it to a website, or distribute it by any other means without permission.

First edition

*This book was professionally typeset on Reedsy.
Find out more at reedsy.com*

Contents

I   Part One

1   The Apparition of Our Lady   3
- Historical background and context   3
  - Spanish Colonization of Mexico   3
  - Indigenous Beliefs and Practices   4
  - Syncretism and Religious Blending   4
  - Early Catholicism in Mexico   5
  - Marian Devotion in Mexico   5
  - Setting the Stage for the Apparitions   5
- The story of Juan Diego   7
  - First Encounter with the Virgin Mary   7
  - The Bishop's Skepticism   8
  - The Miraculous Image   8
  - The Conversion of the Bishop   9
  - Confirmation of the Apparitions   9
  - The Tilma and the Basilica   10
  - Juan Diego's Legacy   11
- Description of the apparitions   11
- Messages conveyed by Our Lady   14

2   Miracles and Conversions   17
- Miracles associated with Our Lady of Guadalupe   17
  - The Miraculous Image   17

Juan Diego's Uncle's Healing	18
Conversion of the Indigenous Population	18
Protection from Spanish Conquest	19
Miracles of Healing and Favors Granted	19
Miracles of Preservation	19
- Impact of the apparitions on indigenous peoples: Conversion of millions to Christianity	20

II Part Two

3 Understanding the Novena	27
- Definition and purpose of a novena	27
- Why pray a novena to Our Lady of Guadalupe?	30
- Benefits and blessings of the novena devotion	32
4 Preparation for the Novena	36
- Setting the right mindset and intentions	36
- Importance of faith and trust	39
- Choosing the right time and place for prayer	42
5 The Nine Days of Novena	45
- Day 1: Praying for Love and Unity	45
- Day 2: Praying for Hope and Healing	46
- Day 3: Praying for Faith and Strength	46
- Day 4: Praying for Family and Relationships	47
- Day 5: Praying for Peace and Reconciliation	47
- Day 6: Praying for Guidance and Wisdom	48
- Day 7: Praying for Joy and Gratitude	49
- Day 8: Praying for Forgiveness and Mercy	49
- Day 9: Praying for Salvation and Eternal Life	50
6 Additional Prayers and Devotions	51
- Prayers for special intentions	51

I

Part One

Biography of Our Lady of Guadalupe

1

The Apparition of Our Lady

- Historical background and context

Spanish Colonization of Mexico

The historical background and context of the apparition of Our Lady of Guadalupe begin with the arrival of Spanish explorers and conquistadors in Mexico in the early 16th century. Led by Hernán Cortés, the Spanish expedition arrived in 1519, seeking to expand Spanish influence and acquire wealth in the New World. Over time, the Spanish gained control over the Aztec Empire, led by Emperor Moctezuma II, and established the colony of New Spain.

Indigenous Beliefs and Practices

Prior to the arrival of the Spanish, Mexico was home to various indigenous civilizations with rich spiritual beliefs and practices. The Aztecs, in particular, had a complex religious system centered around their pantheon of gods. One prominent figure was Tonantzin, a revered mother goddess associated with fertility and the earth. The worship of Tonantzin was deeply ingrained in the Aztec culture and held great significance for the indigenous population.

Syncretism and Religious Blending

With the Spanish conquest and the introduction of Christianity, a process of syncretism began to take place. Syncretism refers to the blending of different religious beliefs and practices. The Spanish missionaries, in their efforts to convert the indigenous peoples, incorporated elements of the native traditions into the Christian faith. This blending allowed for a sense of continuity and familiarity for the indigenous population, making the transition to Christianity more accessible.

Early Catholicism in Mexico

Following the conquest, Catholicism became the dominant religion in Mexico. The Spanish authorities, along with the Catholic Church, worked to establish a strong Catholic presence and hierarchy in the region. Churches, monasteries, and cathedrals were built, and religious orders were established to administer the sacraments and spread the faith. The veneration of saints, particularly the Virgin Mary, played a central role in the religious life of the colonial society.

Marian Devotion in Mexico

Marian devotion held a special place in the hearts of the Mexican people. The indigenous peoples had a deep reverence for motherhood and femininity, which resonated with the veneration of the Virgin Mary. The Spanish missionaries encouraged the devotion to Mary, presenting her as a compassionate and loving intercessor between God and humanity. Marian shrines and images became focal points of devotion throughout Mexico, attracting pilgrims and inspiring profound faith.

Setting the Stage for the Apparitions

By the early 16th century, the indigenous population had experienced significant upheaval and upheaval due to the Spanish conquest. Many aspects of their traditional culture and religious practices had been suppressed or destroyed, leaving a void that yearned to be filled. The introduction of Catholicism provided a new framework for spirituality, but there was still a need for a connection that resonated with their cultural identity.

In this context, the apparitions of Our Lady of Guadalupe played a crucial role in bridging the gap between the indigenous population and the Catholic faith. The apparitions offered a profound encounter with the divine that was both deeply spiritual and culturally relevant. The appearance of the Virgin Mary as a mestiza woman, speaking to Juan Diego in his native language of Nahuatl, affirmed the dignity and worth of the indigenous peoples and acknowledged their place within the Catholic faith.

Furthermore, the timing of the apparitions was significant. They occurred in December 1531, during the season of the Aztec feast of Tonantzin, which was celebrated around the winter solstice. This temporal connection added to the appeal and legitimacy of the apparitions for the indigenous population, as it aligned with their existing cultural practices.

The historical background and context of the apparition of Our Lady of Guadalupe demonstrate the convergence of indigenous beliefs, Spanish colonization, and Catholicism in Mexico. The apparitions provided a profound spiritual experience that not only united the diverse population but also validated and celebrated their unique cultural heritage. The events of Guadalupe became a pivotal moment in Mexican history, serving as a symbol of unity, faith, and the enduring presence of the Virgin

Mary as the Mother of all peoples.

- The story of Juan Diego

The story of Our Lady of Guadalupe revolves around a humble indigenous man named Juan Diego. Juan Diego was born in 1474 in Cuauhtitlán, a small village near Mexico City. He belonged to the Chichimeca people and was raised in the Aztec tradition. As a devout Christian, Juan Diego embraced the Catholic faith and was known for his piety and humility.

First Encounter with the Virgin Mary

On December 9, 1531, Juan Diego had a life-changing encounter with the Virgin Mary on Tepeyac Hill, near Mexico City. As he was walking to attend Mass, he heard celestial music and saw a radiant light. Juan Diego was astonished to find himself in the presence of a beautiful woman who identified herself as the "Ever-Virgin Holy Mary, Mother of God."

The Virgin Mary spoke to Juan Diego in his native language of Nahuatl and conveyed her desire for a church to be built on the site. She entrusted him with a mission to visit the bishop and deliver her message. Filled with awe and reverence, Juan Diego agreed to carry out her request.

The Bishop's Skepticism

Juan Diego promptly went to the residence of Bishop Juan de Zumárraga and shared the extraordinary encounter with the Virgin Mary. Initially, the bishop was skeptical and requested proof of the apparition. Understanding the bishop's hesitation, Juan Diego returned to Tepeyac Hill to seek the Virgin Mary's guidance.

The Miraculous Image

On December 12, 1531, Juan Diego encountered the Virgin Mary once again on Tepeyac Hill. He expressed his difficulty in convincing the bishop and asked for a sign. In response, the Virgin Mary instructed Juan Diego to gather flowers from the barren hilltop and present them to the bishop as a miraculous sign.

Following the Virgin Mary's instructions, Juan Diego found an abundance of beautiful Castilian roses, which were not native to the region. He gathered them in his cloak, known as a tilma, and carried them to the bishop. When Juan Diego opened his tilma to present the roses, a miraculous image of the Virgin Mary appeared imprinted on the fabric.

The Conversion of the Bishop

Upon seeing the miraculous image and hearing Juan Diego's account, Bishop Zumárraga was filled with awe and recognized the authenticity of the apparitions. He realized that this was a divine sign and that the Virgin Mary had chosen Tepeyac Hill as a sacred place.

The bishop acknowledged the significance of the apparitions and expressed his commitment to fulfill the Virgin Mary's request for a church to be built. He instructed Juan Diego to return to Tepeyac Hill and ask the Virgin Mary for a sign that would confirm her presence and obtain her final approval.

Confirmation of the Apparitions

Juan Diego returned to Tepeyac Hill, where the Virgin Mary awaited him. She revealed herself as Our Lady of Guadalupe, a title that would forever be associated with the apparitions. The Virgin Mary assured Juan Diego that she would grant his request for a sign that would convince the bishop.

The following day, December 12, Juan Diego's uncle became gravely ill. Filled with worry and unable to seek the priest's help, Juan Diego took a different route to avoid encountering the Virgin Mary. However, the Virgin Mary appeared to him and assured him of his uncle's recovery. She also instructed Juan Diego to climb the hill and gather flowers as another miraculous sign.

When Juan Diego reached the top of the hill, he found an array of beautiful flowers, including Castilian roses. He carefully gathered them in his tilma and returned to the Virgin Mary. She rearranged the flowers, ensuring they wouldn't fall out, and instructed Juan Diego to present them to the bishop as a sign.

The Tilma and the Basilica

Juan Diego hurried back to the bishop's residence and unfolded his tilma in the presence of Bishop Zumárraga. As the roses cascaded to the floor, the miraculous image of Our Lady of Guadalupe appeared on the tilma. The bishop and those present fell to their knees in awe and wonder, recognizing the divine nature of the image.

The image on the tilma, now known as the Our Lady of Guadalupe image, became a powerful symbol of faith and conversion. The bishop fulfilled the Virgin Mary's request and oversaw the construction of a church on Tepeyac Hill, the Basilica of Our Lady of Guadalupe, which stands to this day as one of the most important pilgrimage sites in the world.

Juan Diego's Legacy

After the apparitions, Juan Diego dedicated his life to spreading the message of Our Lady of Guadalupe and caring for the shrine. He became a revered figure among the indigenous population and was recognized for his unwavering faith, humility, and devotion. Juan Diego's tilma, bearing the miraculous image, remains preserved and displayed in the Basilica of Our Lady of Guadalupe, serving as a testament to his role in this extraordinary event.

The story of Juan Diego is a testament to the transformative power of faith and the profound encounter with the Virgin Mary. His obedience, humility, and unwavering commitment to carrying out the Virgin Mary's message continue to inspire millions of believers worldwide.

- Description of the apparitions

The apparitions of Our Lady of Guadalupe to Juan Diego began on December 9, 1531, on Tepeyac Hill near Mexico City. Juan Diego, while on his way to attend Mass, encountered a radiant light and heard celestial music. To his astonishment, he found himself in the presence of a beautiful woman who identified herself as the "Ever-Virgin Holy Mary, Mother of God."

During the first apparition, the Virgin Mary spoke to Juan Diego in his native Nahuatl language, demonstrating her compassion and desire to be understood by the indigenous people. She expressed her concern for the well-being of all her children and requested that a church be built in her honor on Tepeyac Hill.

The Second Apparition

After the initial encounter, Juan Diego hurried to the residence of Bishop Juan de Zumárraga to deliver the message from the Virgin Mary. The bishop, initially skeptical, requested a sign to validate the authenticity of the apparitions. Upon returning to Tepeyac Hill, Juan Diego met the Virgin Mary once again.

During the second apparition, the Virgin Mary reassured Juan Diego of her presence and instructed him to return to the bishop with a miraculous sign. She directed him to gather flowers from the barren hilltop. To Juan Diego's surprise, he found an abundance of beautiful Castilian roses, which were not native to the region.

The Miraculous Image

Juan Diego gathered the roses in his tilma, a cloak made of coarse fabric. As he presented the roses to the bishop, he opened his tilma, and to everyone's astonishment, a miraculous image of the Virgin Mary appeared imprinted on the fabric. The image on the tilma, now famously known as the Our Lady of Guadalupe image, captivated all who saw it.

The image depicts a young woman with indigenous features, dressed in a gown adorned with stars, standing on a crescent moon. The Virgin Mary's hands are joined in prayer, and her eyes are cast downward in a gesture of humility and compassion. The image radiates a sense of love, serenity, and maternal care.

What is particularly remarkable about the image is its incorruptibility and the vividness of its colors despite being on a fragile and coarse fabric. The preservation of the image over centuries has been a source of wonder and awe, with scientists unable to explain its origin and enduring qualities.

The Third and Final Apparition

Following the bishop's request for further confirmation, Juan Diego returned to Tepeyac Hill and encountered the Virgin Mary for the third and final time. During this apparition, the Virgin Mary assured Juan Diego of his uncle's recovery from illness and provided him with the final sign for the bishop.

She instructed Juan Diego to climb the hill and gather flowers, which he did. The Virgin Mary rearranged the flowers in his tilma, ensuring they wouldn't fall out. Juan Diego then returned to the bishop and, upon opening his tilma, the miraculous image was revealed, solidifying the bishop's belief in the apparitions.

The apparitions of Our Lady of Guadalupe to Juan Diego were marked by the Virgin Mary's gentle and compassionate presence, her messages of love and care for all her children, and the extraordinary signs and miracles associated with the encounters. The miraculous image on Juan Diego's tilma continues to inspire and captivate people of all backgrounds, serving as a powerful symbol of faith, unity, and divine intervention.

- Messages conveyed by Our Lady

One of the central messages conveyed by Our Lady of Guadalupe is the boundless love and compassion she holds for all her children. Through her apparitions to Juan Diego, she demonstrated her deep concern for the well-being of the people and her desire to alleviate their suffering. The Virgin Mary's presence and words conveyed a sense of maternal love, assuring all that they are cherished and cared for by a compassionate and merciful mother.

Unity and Harmony

Our Lady of Guadalupe emphasized the importance of unity and harmony among people. By appearing as a mestiza woman, with features that resonated with both the indigenous and Spanish populations, she symbolized the coming together of different cultures and backgrounds. Her message transcended divisions and called for reconciliation, understanding, and respect among all people, regardless of their differences.

Conversion and Faith

The Virgin Mary urged the indigenous people and all who encountered her message to embrace the Catholic faith and convert to Christianity. Her appearance as a divine figure, speaking in their native language and understanding their cultural context, served as a bridge between their traditional beliefs and the new faith. She encouraged the people to turn to God, seek forgiveness, and live lives rooted in faith, hope, and love.

The Importance of Prayer and Devotion

Throughout the apparitions, Our Lady of Guadalupe emphasized the significance of prayer and devotion. She encouraged Juan Diego and all believers to engage in fervent prayer, both individually and as a community. The Virgin Mary presented herself as a powerful intercessor, advocating for the needs and intentions of the people and encouraging them to approach God with a humble and open heart.

Protection and Miracles

Our Lady of Guadalupe assured the people of her protection and the miracles that would flow from their faith. She promised to be a source of comfort and refuge, offering her maternal care and intercession in times of difficulty. The miraculous image imprinted on Juan Diego's tilma served as a tangible manifestation of her presence and divine intervention, inspiring awe and deepening the faith of believers.

Motherhood and Dignity

The Virgin Mary, as Our Lady of Guadalupe, emphasized the sacredness of motherhood and the dignity of all human life. Her appearance as a nurturing mother figure, symbolized by her pregnancy and the tender care she exhibited, affirmed the importance of women and their role in society. She embraced the marginalized, the oppressed, and the vulnerable, offering them hope, solace, and a reminder of their inherent worth.

The messages conveyed by Our Lady of Guadalupe through her apparitions to Juan Diego continue to resonate with believers worldwide. They emphasize love, unity, conversion, prayer, protection, and the recognition of the dignity of all people. Her messages inspire faith, foster a sense of belonging, and call individuals and communities to live lives rooted in compassion, justice, and spiritual devotion.

2

Miracles and Conversions

- Miracles associated with Our Lady of Guadalupe

The apparitions of Our Lady of Guadalupe to Juan Diego were accompanied by numerous miracles, both during and after the events at Tepeyac Hill. These miracles serve as powerful testimonies to the divine intervention and intercession of the Virgin Mary. They have inspired awe and faith in countless individuals and have contributed to the enduring significance of Our Lady of Guadalupe.

The Miraculous Image

The most notable and enduring miracle associated with Our Lady of Guadalupe is the miraculous image imprinted on Juan Diego's tilma. The image has defied scientific explanation and remains preserved to this day, despite the passage of centuries. It is believed to possess supernatural qualities, including incorruptibility and the ability to emit inexplicable radiance.

Juan Diego's Uncle's Healing

During one of the apparitions, the Virgin Mary assured Juan Diego of his uncle's recovery from a severe illness. Following her instructions, Juan Diego found his uncle restored to health, which was seen as a miraculous healing attributed to the intercession of Our Lady of Guadalupe.

Conversion of the Indigenous Population

The apparitions of Our Lady of Guadalupe led to a profound and widespread conversion of the indigenous population of Mexico. The miraculous image on Juan Diego's tilma, along with the messages of love, compassion, and unity conveyed by the Virgin Mary, touched the hearts of countless individuals. Many abandoned their traditional beliefs and embraced the Catholic faith, leading to a transformative spiritual awakening and a deepening of their relationship with God.

Protection from Spanish Conquest

The devotion to Our Lady of Guadalupe became a symbol of resistance and protection during the tumultuous period of Spanish conquest in Mexico. The indigenous people saw the Virgin Mary as their advocate and protector, and they attributed various instances of deliverance and victory to her intercession. These accounts of protection further fueled devotion to Our Lady of Guadalupe and solidified her significance in Mexican history and culture.

Miracles of Healing and Favors Granted

Over the centuries, numerous miraculous healings and favors have been attributed to the intercession of Our Lady of Guadalupe. Devotees recount stories of physical healings, spiritual transformations, and answered prayers. These personal miracles serve as a testament to the powerful intercessory role that Our Lady of Guadalupe continues to play in the lives of believers.

Miracles of Preservation

The preservation of the miraculous image on Juan Diego's tilma is itself considered a continuous and ongoing miracle. Despite its exposure to the elements and various attempts at deterioration, the image remains vibrant and intact. Scientists and experts have been unable to explain the origin of the colors, the lack of natural pigments, and the extraordinary preservation of the fabric over centuries.

The miracles associated with Our Lady of Guadalupe bear witness to the supernatural presence and intervention of the Virgin Mary. They affirm the belief that she continues to intercede on behalf of those who seek her assistance, offering solace, healing, and protection. These miracles have deepened faith, inspired devotion, and served as a source of hope and encouragement for generations of believers.

- Impact of the apparitions on indigenous peoples: Conversion of millions to Christianity

The apparitions of Our Lady of Guadalupe had a profound impact on the indigenous peoples of Mexico, leading to the conversion of millions to Christianity. The encounters between the Virgin Mary and Juan Diego resonated deeply with the indigenous population, offering a bridge between their traditional beliefs and the Catholic faith. The messages of love, unity, and compassion conveyed by Our Lady of Guadalupe struck a chord with the indigenous peoples, transforming their spiritual landscape.

Cultural Relevance and Acceptance

One of the key factors that facilitated the conversion of indigenous peoples was the cultural relevance and acceptance embedded within the apparitions. The Virgin Mary appeared as a mestiza woman, embracing both indigenous and Spanish elements. This depiction allowed the indigenous population to see themselves represented in the divine figure, establishing a sense of belonging and cultural recognition.

Integration of Indigenous Beliefs

The apparitions of Our Lady of Guadalupe incorporated elements of indigenous beliefs, practices, and symbolism. The use of Nahuatl, the native language of Juan Diego, and the indigenous context in which the apparitions took place demonstrated the Virgin Mary's understanding and respect for the indigenous culture. This integration helped the indigenous peoples see connections between their own spirituality and the Catholic faith, facilitating a smoother transition and fostering a sense of continuity.

Messages of Love and Compassion

The messages of love and compassion conveyed by Our Lady of Guadalupe deeply resonated with the indigenous peoples, who had endured oppression and marginalization during the Spanish conquest. The Virgin Mary's affirmation of their dignity, her call for unity and harmony, and her promise of protection and intercession touched their hearts and offered a renewed sense of hope and purpose.

Recognition and Empowerment

The apparitions of Our Lady of Guadalupe played a significant role in recognizing the worth and value of the indigenous peoples. The Virgin Mary's choice to appear to Juan Diego, an indigenous man, and her emphasis on his role as her messenger elevated the status of the indigenous population, empowering them with a sense of purpose and divine significance. This recognition fostered a positive self-image and contributed to a newfound pride in their cultural heritage.

Social and Spiritual Transformation

The conversion of millions of indigenous peoples to Christianity brought about a significant social and spiritual transformation. As they embraced the Catholic faith, the indigenous population integrated into the broader Christian community, forming new bonds and connections. This integration led to the establishment of vibrant indigenous Christian communities, which became centers for cultural preservation, spiritual growth, and social empowerment.

Devotion and Pilgrimage

The devotion to Our Lady of Guadalupe became deeply rooted in the indigenous culture of Mexico. The apparitions gave rise to a strong tradition of pilgrimage to the Basilica of Our Lady of Guadalupe, where millions of indigenous peoples and believers from around the world gather to honor and seek the intercession of the Virgin Mary. These pilgrimages serve as powerful expressions of faith, unity, and cultural identity.

The impact of the apparitions on indigenous peoples is undeniable. The conversion of millions to Christianity, the integration of indigenous beliefs, the recognition of dignity, and the empowerment of indigenous communities have shaped the spiritual and cultural landscape of Mexico. The apparitions of Our Lady of Guadalupe continue to inspire and transform the lives of indigenous peoples, reminding them of their innate worth and their place in the story of faith and salvation.

II

Part Two

The Novena Devotion

3

Understanding the Novena

- Definition and purpose of a novena

A novena is a form of Catholic devotion that consists of a series of prayers or spiritual exercises repeated over nine consecutive days. The word "novena" is derived from the Latin word "novem," meaning "nine." Novenas are a rich tradition in Catholicism and are practiced to seek divine intervention, express devotion, and deepen one's spiritual connection with God and the saints.

Purpose of a Novena

The purpose of a novena varies depending on the intention and focus of the prayers. Some common purposes of a novena include:

Petitionary Prayers: Novenas are often used as a way to make specific requests or seek intercession for particular needs or intentions. Believers may pray a novena to ask for healing, guidance, comfort, protection, or any other specific intention. It is believed that by persevering in prayer for nine consecutive days, one demonstrates faith, perseverance, and a deep desire for God's response.

Preparation for Feasts and Solemnities: Novenas are frequently employed as a form of spiritual preparation for important feasts and solemnities in the Catholic liturgical calendar. These novenas provide an opportunity to reflect, meditate, and draw closer to the central themes and mysteries associated with the upcoming celebration. For example, a novena may be prayed before Christmas, Easter, or the feast day of a particular saint.

Devotional Practices: Novenas are also practiced as acts of devotion to honor and seek the intercession of saints, particularly the Blessed Virgin Mary. Believers may pray novenas to express their love, gratitude, and veneration for a particular saint, seeking their guidance, protection, or special favors. Novenas dedicated to Our Lady of Guadalupe, for example, are popular among those seeking her intercession.

Spiritual Growth and Transformation: Novenas provide a structured and focused period of prayer and reflection, encouraging individuals to deepen their relationship with God and grow in their faith. Through consistent prayer over nine days, one can cultivate a habit of daily prayer, foster a spirit of perseverance, and open their heart to the movement of the Holy Spirit. Novenas can serve as a means to nurture spiritual growth, seek clarity, and experience personal transformation.

Structure of a Novena

Novenas typically follow a prescribed structure, although variations exist. The structure generally involves the following elements:

Opening Prayer: Each day of the novena begins with an opening prayer, often invoking the Holy Spirit and setting the tone for the prayers and reflections that follow.

Daily Prayer or Reflection: Each day of the novena includes a specific prayer or reflection that focuses on the intention or theme of the novena. These prayers may be composed prayers, passages from Scripture, or meditations that help individuals engage with the spiritual purpose of the novena.

Petitions or Personal Prayers: After the designated prayer or reflection, individuals may include their personal petitions, bringing their specific needs and intentions before God or the interceding saint.

Closing Prayer: Each day of the novena concludes with a closing prayer, expressing gratitude, seeking God's grace, or offering praise and worship.

Continuity and Perseverance: The novena is repeated over nine consecutive days, maintaining the rhythm and structure of the prayers. The act of persevering in prayer for this designated period reinforces the importance of commitment, faith, and trust in God's timing and response.

Novenas provide a powerful avenue for prayer, reflection, and spiritual connection. They allow individuals to express their deepest desires, seek divine guidance, and grow in faith. Whether for petition, devotion, preparation, or personal transformation, novenas serve as a valuable tool in the spiritual journey of believers.

- Why pray a novena to Our Lady of Guadalupe?

Praying a novena to Our Lady of Guadalupe holds a special significance for many believers. Our Lady of Guadalupe is an important figure in Catholicism, particularly in Mexico and Latin America, where devotion to her is deeply rooted. Here are some reasons why individuals choose to pray a novena to Our Lady of Guadalupe:

Seeking Intercession and Assistance

One of the primary reasons to pray a novena to Our Lady of Guadalupe is to seek her intercession and assistance. Believers turn to her as a powerful advocate, trusting in her maternal care and her ability to bring their intentions before God. They believe that by praying a novena to Our Lady of Guadalupe, she will intercede on their behalf, presenting their needs, desires, and concerns to God and obtaining graces and favors for them.

Protection and Guidance

Our Lady of Guadalupe is often seen as a source of protection and guidance. Praying a novena to her is a way of seeking her motherly protection and guidance in times of difficulty, uncertainty, or danger. Individuals may turn to her for physical protection, spiritual strength, or guidance in making important decisions. They trust that through their prayers, Our Lady of Guadalupe will surround them with her loving care and lead them on the right path.

Deepening Faith and Connection

Praying a novena to Our Lady of Guadalupe can also serve as a means of deepening one's faith and connection with God. The devotion and perseverance involved in a novena provide an opportunity for individuals to cultivate a more intimate relationship with Our Lady of Guadalupe and grow in their trust and reliance on her intercession. Through this process, believers often experience a deepening of their faith, a heightened sense of spiritual connection, and a greater awareness of God's presence in their lives.

Honoring and Expressing Gratitude

Novenas to Our Lady of Guadalupe are also a way to honor her and express gratitude for her presence and intercession. Believers may pray a novena as an act of thanksgiving for answered prayers, blessings received, or specific graces granted through her intercession. By dedicating nine days of prayer and reflection, individuals can express their love, veneration, and appreciation for Our Lady of Guadalupe's role in their lives.

Communal Devotion and Cultural Identity

Praying a novena to Our Lady of Guadalupe is often a communal devotion, bringing people together in shared faith and devotion. This devotion serves as a unifying force, fostering a sense of community and cultural identity, particularly among Mexican and Latin American Catholics. Participating in a novena allows individuals to connect with others who share the same devotion and to collectively honor and seek the intercession of Our Lady of Guadalupe.

In summary, praying a novena to Our Lady of Guadalupe offers believers a means to seek her intercession, find protection and guidance, deepen their faith, express gratitude, and participate in a communal devotion. The devotion to Our Lady of Guadalupe holds deep cultural and spiritual significance, drawing countless individuals to turn to her in prayer and entrust their needs to her loving care.

- Benefits and blessings of the novena devotion

Strengthening Faith

One of the significant benefits of the novena devotion is the strengthening of faith. Through the consistent practice of praying a novena, individuals develop a habit of regular prayer and deepening their relationship with God. The focused and intentional nature of the novena allows believers to immerse themselves in prayer, reflection, and meditation, leading to a more profound faith and trust in God's providence.

Deepening Spiritual Connection

The novena devotion provides an opportunity to deepen one's spiritual connection with God and the saints. By dedicating nine consecutive days to prayer and reflection, individuals create a sacred space for encountering the divine presence. This focused time allows for a more profound sense of communion with God, fostering a deeper understanding of His will and a heightened awareness of His guidance in their lives.

Answered Prayers

Praying a novena can bring about answered prayers and blessings. The consistent and persevering nature of the novena demonstrates one's sincere and persistent trust in God's providence. Believers often testify to the efficacy of the novena devotion, sharing stories of prayers answered and graces received as a result of their dedicated nine days of prayer. While God's timing and response may vary, the novena devotion invites individuals to trust in His wisdom and rely on His divine intervention.

Spiritual Discernment

Engaging in a novena devotion can aid in spiritual discernment. The extended period of focused prayer and reflection allows individuals to seek clarity and guidance in making important decisions or discerning God's will in their lives. Through the novena, believers can open their hearts to the promptings of the Holy Spirit, seeking discernment and wisdom in navigating life's challenges and choices.

Increased Gratitude and Appreciation

Practicing the novena devotion cultivates a spirit of gratitude and appreciation. By dedicating nine days to prayer, individuals have the opportunity to reflect on God's blessings, express gratitude for His goodness, and acknowledge His presence in their lives. The novena devotion encourages believers to develop a thankful disposition and to recognize the many ways in which God blesses them.

Spiritual Growth and Transformation

The novena devotion can lead to significant spiritual growth and transformation. By engaging in consistent prayer, reflection, and meditation, individuals deepen their understanding of their faith, encounter God's grace, and experience personal transformation. The novena journey allows believers to develop virtues such as patience, perseverance, humility, and trust, contributing to their overall spiritual development.

Community and Communal Prayer

Participating in a novena devotion often fosters a sense of community and shared prayer. Many individuals join together in praying the same novena, either in physical communities or through online platforms. This communal aspect of the novena provides a sense of unity, support, and shared faith. Believers can come together, supporting and encouraging one another on their spiritual journey.

The novena devotion offers numerous benefits and blessings to those who engage in it. It strengthens faith, deepens spiritual connection, brings about answered prayers, aids in spiritual discernment, cultivates gratitude and appreciation, facilitates spiritual growth and transformation, and fosters community and communal prayer. Through the dedicated practice of the novena, believers can experience the richness of the spiritual journey and draw closer to God and His divine grace.

4

Preparation for the Novena

- Setting the right mindset and intentions

Understanding the Importance of Mindset and Intentions

Preparing for a novena involves more than just the practical aspects of gathering prayers and materials. It also requires setting the right mindset and intentions. The mindset we bring and the intentions we set lay the foundation for a fruitful and meaningful novena experience. Here are some key considerations for setting the right mindset and intentions:

Cultivating a Spirit of Openness and Surrender

To prepare for a novena, it is essential to cultivate a spirit of openness and surrender to God's will. This mindset involves letting go of personal agendas and desires and placing trust in God's wisdom and guidance. By surrendering our will to God, we create space for His plans and purposes to unfold throughout the novena.

Reflecting on the Purpose and Intention of the Novena

Before beginning a novena, take time to reflect on its purpose and intention. Ask yourself why you are embarking on this spiritual journey and what you hope to gain from it. It could be seeking guidance in a particular area of life, seeking healing, or expressing gratitude. Clarifying your intentions will help you stay focused and engaged throughout the nine days of prayer.

Examining the State of Your Heart

As you prepare for the novena, take a moment to examine the state of your heart. Are there any areas where you need healing, forgiveness, or reconciliation? Are there any obstacles that hinder your relationship with God or others? Use this time to seek inner healing, to forgive and seek forgiveness, and to purify your heart. A repentant and open heart creates a fertile ground for God's grace to work during the novena.

Seeking Guidance from Scripture and Spiritual Resources

Drawing inspiration from Scripture and other spiritual resources can help set the right mindset and intentions. Read passages that relate to the intention of your novena and meditate on their message. Seek guidance from trusted spiritual mentors, books, or online resources that can provide insights and reflections relevant to your novena's purpose. This will deepen your understanding and bring clarity to your intentions.

Praying for Clarity and Discernment

Pray for clarity and discernment as you prepare for the novena. Seek God's guidance in understanding His will and aligning your intentions with His purposes. Ask the Holy Spirit to enlighten your mind and heart, enabling you to discern the intentions that are in harmony with God's plan for your life.

Cultivating a Spirit of Gratitude

Gratitude is a powerful mindset to cultivate before and during a novena. Recognize and appreciate the blessings and graces you have received in your life. Express gratitude to God for His love, mercy, and faithfulness. Gratitude opens our hearts to receive more fully the blessings God desires to bestow upon us during the novena.

Setting Specific and Sincere Intentions

Be specific and sincere in setting your intentions for the novena. Identify the areas of your life or the specific needs you wish to bring before God. Frame your intentions in clear and concise language, expressing them with heartfelt sincerity. Remember that God knows the deepest desires of your heart, but articulating them in prayer helps to focus your mind and strengthens your intention.

Praying for God's Will to Be Done

Finally, as you set your intentions, always pray for God's will to be done. While it is important to bring our desires and needs before God, we must also acknowledge His sovereignty and trust in His wisdom. Surrender your intentions to God's divine plan and pray that His will, which is perfect and loving, be accomplished in your life.

Setting the right mindset and intentions before beginning a novena is crucial for a meaningful and transformative experience. Cultivating a spirit of openness and surrender, reflecting on the purpose and intention of the novena, examining the state of your heart, seeking guidance from Scripture and spiritual resources, praying for clarity and discernment, cultivating gratitude, setting specific and sincere intentions, and praying for God's will to be done are essential steps in preparing for the novena. These practices create a fertile ground for God's grace to work, aligning our hearts and minds with His divine purposes.

- Importance of faith and trust

Faith as the Foundation

Faith plays a fundamental role in preparing for a novena. It is through faith that we approach God, believing in His presence, His love, and His power to answer our prayers. Without faith, the novena becomes a mere ritual or empty practice. By cultivating and nurturing our faith, we open ourselves to the transformative work of God during the novena.

Trusting in God's Providence

Trust is closely intertwined with faith and is essential in preparing for a novena. Trusting in God's providence means surrendering our worries, anxieties, and uncertainties to Him. It involves acknowledging that God has a perfect plan for our lives and that He is intimately involved in every aspect. Trust enables us to rely on God's wisdom, goodness, and timing, even when things seem uncertain or challenging.

Letting Go of Control

Preparing for a novena requires letting go of control and surrendering to God's will. Often, we have our own ideas of how our prayers should be answered or our intentions fulfilled. However, true trust means relinquishing our desire for control and placing our complete trust in God's loving guidance. Letting go allows us to invite God's transformative power into our lives and enables us to experience His grace in unexpected and marvelous ways.

Strengthening Faith through Prayer and Scripture

Prayer and Scripture are powerful tools for strengthening our faith and trust in God. Prior to the novena, spend time in prayer, seeking God's presence and guidance. Engage in conversations with Him, expressing your desires, concerns, and intentions, and listening for His still, small voice. Immerse yourself in Scripture, meditating on God's promises, His faithfulness throughout history, and the examples of trust displayed by biblical figures. These practices deepen our faith and reinforce our trust in God's faithfulness.

Remembering Past Faithfulness

Reflecting on past experiences of God's faithfulness can bolster our trust in Him. Recall moments when God answered prayers, provided for your needs, or guided you through difficult times. Remembering His faithfulness in the past strengthens our confidence that He will continue to be faithful in the present and future. By reminding ourselves of His past acts of love and provision, we build a foundation of trust that sustains us during the novena.

Embracing Patience and God's Timing

Faith and trust require patience and an acceptance of God's timing. Sometimes, our prayers may not be answered immediately or in the way we expect. However, cultivating patience and trusting in God's perfect timing allows us to remain steadfast in our faith. Recognize that God's plan may unfold differently from our own, but His timing is always perfect. Trusting in His timing enables us to surrender to His greater wisdom and embrace His plan with a willing heart.

Seeking Support from the Faith Community

The faith community can provide valuable support in strengthening our faith and trust. Engage with fellow believers, join prayer groups, or participate in church activities where you can share your intentions, seek encouragement, and pray together. Surrounding yourself with like-minded individuals who share your faith journey can provide comfort, guidance, and accountability as you prepare for the novena.

Faith and trust are indispensable in preparing for a novena.

Faith establishes the foundation for our prayers, while trust enables us to surrender control, embrace God's providence, and patiently await His timing. Strengthening our faith through prayer, Scripture, and remembering past faithfulness reinforces our trust in God's love and faithfulness. Embracing patience and seeking support from the faith community further nourishes our faith and trust, allowing us to approach the novena with a steadfast and confident heart.

- Choosing the right time and place for prayer

Recognizing the Sacredness of Time and Space

When preparing for a novena, it is important to recognize the sacredness of time and space. Choosing the right time and place for prayer can create an environment conducive to deepening your connection with God. By intentionally selecting a suitable time and a dedicated space, you create a sacred atmosphere that enhances your focus, devotion, and receptivity to God's presence.

Finding a Quiet and Distraction-Free Environment

Selecting a quiet and distraction-free environment is vital for prayer during the novena. Find a place where you can minimize external distractions and noise, allowing you to fully immerse yourself in prayer. This could be a quiet corner in your home, a peaceful outdoor setting, or a designated prayer room where you can retreat and find solitude.

Establishing Consistency and Routine

Establishing consistency and routine in your prayer time contributes to a more fruitful novena experience. Choose a time of day that works best for you, where you can dedicate yourself fully to prayer without feeling rushed or interrupted. By making prayer a regular part of your daily routine, you create a habit that deepens your spiritual connection and sustains your commitment to the novena.

Aligning with Natural Rhythms and Personal Energy Levels

Consider aligning your prayer time with natural rhythms and your personal energy levels. Some individuals find early morning prayer invigorating and refreshing, while others connect more deeply with God during the quiet hours of the evening. Pay attention to your own biorhythms and energy patterns to determine the optimal time for prayer, ensuring that you are alert, focused, and receptive.

Utilizing Sacred Symbols and Objects

Enhance your prayer space by incorporating sacred symbols and objects that hold personal significance. These could include religious images, icons, candles, rosaries, or any items that help center your mind and heart on the divine. Surrounding yourself with meaningful symbols can inspire and deepen your prayer experience during the novena.

Creating an Atmosphere of Tranquility and Beauty

Foster an atmosphere of tranquility and beauty in your prayer space. Arrange it in a way that promotes a sense of peace and harmony. You may choose to include soft lighting, calming scents, uplifting music, or elements from nature. Creating an environment that nurtures your senses can facilitate a deeper connection with God and enhance your prayer experience.

Seeking Divine Guidance in Choosing the Time and Place

Seek divine guidance in choosing the time and place for prayer. Invite the Holy Spirit to lead you to the most suitable environment that aligns with your intentions for the novena. Pray for discernment and clarity, asking God to guide you to the time and space where you can most effectively encounter His presence and engage in heartfelt prayer.

Choosing the right time and place for prayer during the novena is essential for creating a sacred and conducive environment. Select a quiet and distraction-free space, establish consistency and routine, align with natural rhythms and personal energy levels, incorporate sacred symbols and objects, create an atmosphere of tranquility and beauty, and seek divine guidance in making these choices. By intentionally setting aside a dedicated time and space for prayer, you create a sacred sanctuary where you can fully engage with God during the novena.

5

The Nine Days of Novena

- Day 1: Praying for Love and Unity

In the name of the Father, and of the Son, and of the Holy Spirit.
Amen.

Dearest Lady of Guadalupe, fruitful Mother of holiness, teach me your ways of tenderness and strength. Please accept my humble prayer offered with heartfelt confidence to beg this favor......

Our Father, Hail Mary, Glory.

In the name of the Father, and of the Son, and of the Holy Spirit.
Amen.

- Day 2: Praying for Hope and Healing

In the name of the Father, and of the Son, and of the Holy Spirit. **Amen.**

O Virgin Mary, conceived without sin, I approach your throne of grace to join the ardent adoration of your Mexican followers who address you by the wonderful Aztec name of Guadalupe. Please grant me a strong faith so that I may always carry out the holy will of your Son. May His will be done on earth as it is in heaven.

Our Father, Hail Mary, Glory.

In the name of the Father, and of the Son, and of the Holy Spirit. **Amen.**

- Day 3: Praying for Faith and Strength

In the name of the Father, and of the Son, and of the Holy Spirit. **Amen.**

O Mary, whose Immaculate Heart was wounded by seven swords of anguish, aid me in walking bravely through the jagged thorns that are littered along my road. My prayer is that you would give me the courage to really emulate you. That is all, Mother, I beg you.

Our Father, Hail Mary, Glory.

In the name of the Father, and of the Son, and of the Holy Spirit.
Amen.

- Day 4: Praying for Family and Relationships

In the name of the Father, and of the Son, and of the Holy Spirit.
Amen.

Dearest Virgin of Guadalupe, I beseech you for a strengthened desire to emulate the kindness of your holy Son, to always seek the benefit of those who are in need. I respectfully pray that you grant me this.

Our Father, Hail Mary, Glory.

In the name of the Father, and of the Son, and of the Holy Spirit.
Amen.

- Day 5: Praying for Peace and Reconciliation

In the name of the Father, and of the Son, and of the Holy Spirit.
Amen.

O most holy Mother, I beseech you to gain forgiveness for all my sins, abundant graces to serve your Son more faithfully from now on, and, finally, the grace to glorify Him with you eternally in paradise.

Our Father, Hail Mary, Glory.

In the name of the Father, and of the Son, and of the Holy Spirit. **Amen.**

- Day 6: Praying for Guidance and Wisdom

In the name of the Father, and of the Son, and of the Holy Spirit. **Amen.**

Mary, Mother of Vocations, expand priestly vocations and fill the land with religious homes that will be a source of light and warmth for the world, as well as a safe haven in stormy nights. Beseech your Son to give us a large number of priests and religious. This is what we request of you, Mother.

Our Father, Hail Mary, Glory.

In the name of the Father, and of the Son, and of the Holy Spirit. **Amen.**

Day 7: Praying for Joy and Gratitude

In the name of the Father, and of the Son, and of the Holy Spirit. **Amen.**

We beseech you, O Lady of Guadalupe, that parents live holy lives and teach their children in a Christian way; that youngsters obey and follow their parents' commands; and that all members of the family pray and worship together. This is what we request of you, Mother.

Our Father, Hail Mary, Glory.

In the name of the Father, and of the Son, and of the Holy Spirit. **Amen.**

Day 8: Praying for Forgiveness and Mercy

In the name of the Father, and of the Son, and of the Holy Spirit. **Amen.**

I humble myself before you, O Mother, with a heart full of the most true devotion, to beseech you to obtain for me the grace to perform the obligations of my position in life with loyalty and constancy.

Our father, Hail Mary, Glory.

In the name of the Father, and of the Son, and of the Holy Spirit. **Amen.**

- Day 9: Praying for Salvation and Eternal Life

In the name of the Father, and of the Son, and of the Holy Spirit. **Amen.**

O God, You have been kind to shower unending benefits upon us by placing us under the particular protection of the Most Blessed Virgin Mary. Grant us, your humble servants, the joy of meeting her face to face in paradise, as we delight in honoring her now on earth.

Our Father, Hail Mary, Glory.

In the name of the Father, and of the Son, and of the Holy Spirit. **Amen.**

6

Additional Prayers and Devotions

- Prayers for special intentions

Within the context of the Our Lady of Guadalupe novena, prayers for special intentions offer individuals the opportunity to present their personal needs, desires, and concerns before Our Lady. These prayers acknowledge the unique circumstances and challenges faced by each individual, seeking Our Lady's intercession and assistance in specific areas of life.

Customized Prayers for Personal Intentions

Prayers for special intentions can be customized to address individual needs and circumstances. This allows participants to express their deepest hopes, struggles, and desires in a personal and heartfelt manner. Customized prayers provide a direct channel for individuals to communicate with Our Lady, seeking her guidance, comfort, and support in their specific situations.

Traditional Catholic Prayers for Special Intentions

There are several traditional Catholic prayers that can be offered for special intentions. These prayers have been cherished by the faithful throughout generations and are known for their efficacy and spiritual depth. Some examples include the Prayer to Our Lady of Guadalupe, the Memorare, the Prayer of St. Francis, or the Prayer to St. Jude, among others. These prayers can be adapted to address specific intentions or used as they are, drawing upon the rich tradition of Catholic devotion.

Approach to Praying for Special Intentions

When praying for special intentions, it is important to approach the prayer with sincerity, faith, and trust in Our Lady's intercession. Focus your mind and heart on the specific intention, allowing yourself to enter into a deep conversation with Our Lady. Express your needs, desires, and concerns honestly and with humility, knowing that Our Lady is a loving and compassionate mother who cares for her children.

Persistence and Perseverance in Prayer

Prayers for special intentions may require persistence and perseverance. Sometimes, answers to our prayers may not come immediately or in the way we expect. It is important to trust in God's timing and to continue praying with faith and hope. Our Lady of Guadalupe, known for her unwavering love and care, will intercede on behalf of those who entrust their intentions to her.

Communal Prayer for Special Intentions

Prayers for special intentions can also be offered in a communal setting. Participating in group prayer allows individuals to unite their intentions and seek collective intercession. This form of prayer fosters a sense of community, support, and shared faith, as participants come together to lift up their needs and intentions before Our Lady of Guadalupe.

Conclusion and Blessing

Conclude the topic of prayers for special intentions by emphasizing the importance of personalizing prayers and fostering a deep connection with Our Lady. Encourage individuals to persist in their prayer, trusting in the intercession of Our Lady of Guadalupe. Offer a final blessing, asking for God's grace and guidance in all their intentions and reminding them of Our Lady's love and compassion.

Prayers for special intentions provide a way for individuals to express their personal needs, desires, and concerns to Our Lady of Guadalupe. These prayers can be customized to address individual circumstances or can be traditional Catholic prayers known for their efficacy. It is important to approach these prayers with sincerity, faith, and trust in Our Lady's intercession. Persistence and perseverance in prayer, both individually and in communal settings, are encouraged. Through prayers for special intentions, individuals seek the loving intercession of

Our Lady of Guadalupe in their specific areas of need.

Printed in Great Britain
by Amazon